Emi Iwakiri

beautiful
hand-stitched jewellery

crocheted,
embroidered,
beaded

Emi Iwakiri

beautiful
hand-stitched jewellery

crocheted,
embroidered,
beaded

35 unique projects inspired by Tokyo style

CICO BOOKS

LONDON NEW YORK

Published in 2009 by CICO Books
an imprint of Ryland Peters & Small Ltd
20–21 Jockey's Fields
London WC1R 4BW

www.cicobooks.co.uk

10 9 8 7 6 5 4 3 2 1

A CIP catalogue record for this book is available from the
British Library.

ISBN: 978-1-906525-36-1

Printed in China

Editor Katie Hardwicke
Designer Luis Peral-Aranda
Photographer Becky Maynes
Stylists Nic Jottkandt and Sue Rowlands
Illustrator Stephen Dew

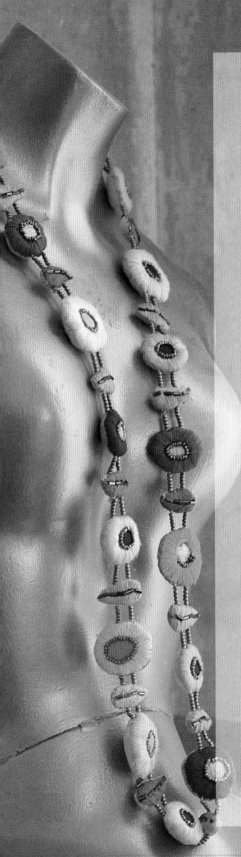

Contents

I really love handicrafts, as I can express my love to people through my work. I feel as though my heart itself is delivered with my work to people. I worked as a stylist for commercial photographers and as a designer of fashion clothing for a long time. I loved and enjoyed my job, but it was a very busy and tiring world. I hoped to make something in which I could express myself and to see the faces of people who wore and enjoyed my work. So, one day, I decided to leave and establish my own studio and haven't regretted my decision for one moment! I now enjoy my life as a crafter and a designer. I plan to move my studio to one of the southern islands of Japan – it is a beautiful island with a coral reef and a lot of greenery and flowers. I can always get inspiration for my work from nature.

Crochet and fabric accessories are wonderful things to fill your wardrobe. They are versatile and help you to express your own sense of fashion. I hope you enjoy making these accessories and jewellery pieces with love, whether they are for your family, friends or yourself. I believe that you feel the link with people and nature with a piece of thread.

Emi Iwakiri

I feel you are delighted,
I see you are smiling,
I listen you are humming,
To get my work of a piece of thread.

Rain makes plants fine,
Wind brings great energy,
Land nurtures them gently,
They can bloom toward the Sun.
Everything links with a piece of thread.

Even a tiny flower can make people happy,
You can do it with a piece of thread.

The projects
in this chapter use
straightforward sewing
skills to create a range of exciting
and individual pieces. With a few
simple embroidery stitches
and using beads and yarns as
embellishments, you can create
some very personal adornments
that will bring colour, style and
texture to your jewellery
collection.

hand-stitched pieces

silk pearl necklace

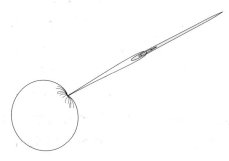

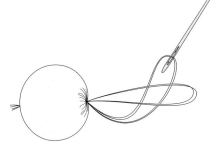

Materials
- ½m (½yd) silk fabric, cream or colour of your choice
- Embroidery needle
- Pearl cotton embroidery thread No. 8, to match the silk fabric
- Wadding

1 Cut out a 5-cm (2-in) square of silk and sew a circle 3.5cm (1⅜in) in diameter in running stitch in the centre. Fold up the edges and stuff the centre with wadding. Pull the thread to close the opening tightly and oversew the opening, trimming the excess thread. Make up 80 'pearl' beads in this manner.

2 To join the beads, thread a needle with double thread. Push the needle through the centre of the first bead and tie a knot to secure it. Stitch through the fabric, make a loop in the thread, then pull the needle through to form a knot.

3 Leave a 5mm (¼in) space between pearls, ensuring that the space is never more than 1cm (⅜in), and continue to join the pearls, knotting closely to the pearl each time to keep them in place. Attach a ring clasp to the end (see page 106) and secure over a pearl to complete the necklace.

Silk and pearls are every girl's favourite! This fantastic necklace combines the two, creating 'pearl' beads from silk, simply strung together to give you a versatile necklace that would look stunning with an elegant dress, or hip and understated with designer jeans. You can use any colour of silk, but pearls in white, cream, black and red will look stylish against any outfit.

This is a great way to recycle loved but worn sweaters – this simple project uses strips cut from a fine wool sweater to create a woolly version of the pearl necklace. Any fine knit sweater would work well – especially one in variegated colours. Thick or hand-knitted sweaters are not suitable.

variation:

red wool *necklace*

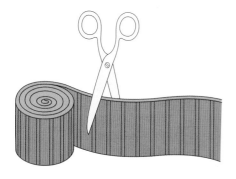

Materials
- Old fine wool sweater
- Pearl cotton embroidery thread No. 8, to match the sweater
- Embroidery needle

1 Cut the sweater into 1-cm (⅜-in) wide strips, across the width, parallel to the stitches. Roll the strip into a ball, approximately 1.5cm (⅝in) in diameter. Trim the excess strip.

2 Sew the edges together, securing the top and bottom ends to make a ball (see Step 1, page 10). Repeat to make 73 wool balls in total. To make the clasp ring, wind the embroidery thread five or six times around a ball to make the loops. Sew around the loops in blanket stitch (see page 107). Join the clasp ring and beads together with a length of embroidery thread, knotting before and after each bead (see Step 3, page 10).

elastic knot necklace

Materials
- 6m (6½yd) elastic cord
- Stranded embroidery thread in different colours
- Embroidery needle
- Sewing thread

1 Cut the elastic cord into 49 lengths of 10cm (4in) and one piece of 1m (40in). Tie a knot at both ends of all the shorter lengths. Fold back the end of the cord.

2 Wind a length of embroidery thread around the knotted end of the cord, approximately 20–25 times, securing the start of the thread beneath the wrapped thread. Trim the end of the thread and tuck it inside the wrapped coil. Repeat the process around the knot at the other end of the elastic cord.

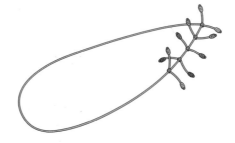

3 With sewing thread, secure the wrapped embroidery thread with a few stitches from the bottom to the top to hold it all in place. Repeat Step 2 approximately five times to build up the knot. Repeat to complete all 49 pieces of elastic.

4 Repeat Steps 2–3 on both ends of the longer length cord. Tie the shorter pieces of the cords along the length of the longer piece. Tie at the neck to secure.

This is the perfect accessory for any busy working woman's wardrobe! You can use it with a navy business suit on Monday, a grey sweater on Tuesday, a good companion for a business trip on Wednesday and Thursday, and with a little black dress for a date on Friday! As this is made of elastic, it is very light and comfortable to wear - you can enjoy it as a single necklace, a double choker and a hair accessory.

This fun necklace is embroidered with musical notes – I feel as though music is dancing around my neck whenever I wear it! Worn with a classic little black dress, it will look mischievous and charming.

musical notes necklace

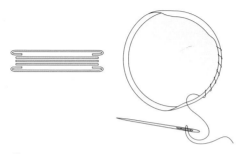

1 Cut out circles from the cotton fabric with the following diameters: for each large disc cut two 26mm/1¹⁄₁₆in (A) and four 25mm/1in (B); for each small disc cut two 23mm/¹⁵⁄₁₆in (C) and four 22mm/⅞in (D). Cut out enough circles to make six large and eight small embroidered discs. Fold over the edges. For the larger discs, sandwich four pieces of B between two layers of A as padding. Whipstitch around them to complete the disc. For the smaller discs, sandwich four pieces of D between two layers of C and whipstitch together.

Materials

- 1m (1yd) white cotton fabric
- Embroidery needle
- Pearl cotton embroidery thread No. 8, black
- 2.50mm crochet hook
- Black seed beads
- 8mm Czech cut beads
- Black bamboo or bugle beads

Embroidery key for 5 designs

25mm (1in)	25mm (1in)	25mm (1in)
	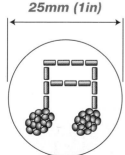	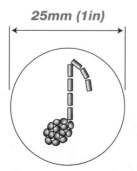

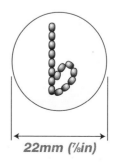

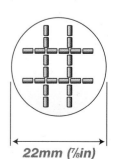

22mm (⅞in)

22mm (⅞in)

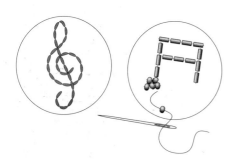

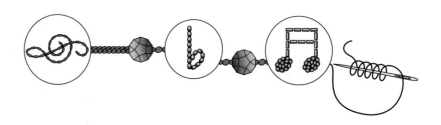

2 Embroider a motif on each disc following the key on page 17. Use small seed beads combined with bamboo or bugle beads, and stitch each motif using a neat running stitch (see page 107). Repeat to make all the discs.

3 Take a large embroidered disc (the clef here), attach the thread through the top edge and knot to secure. Chain stitch (see page 111) approximately five chains, then thread on a bead and knot to secure. Attach the thread to a small disc. Push through and out the opposite side, off centre. Knot the thread by wrapping the thread around the needle several times, attach a bead, knot again and join to the next embroidered disc. Continue until all the embroidered discs are attached with an inner loop, finishing on the inner edge of the final disc. Bring the thread out on the centre of the outer edge of the last disc.

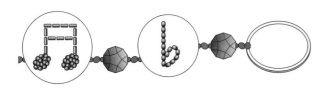

4 Attach a ring clasp (see page 106) at the end of the inside loop.

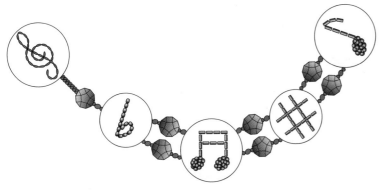

5 Repeat with an outer loop, attaching the beads and discs together as in Step 3, starting from the inner edge of the last disc. As it is longer than the inside loop, adjust the balance with a few more knots in between discs.

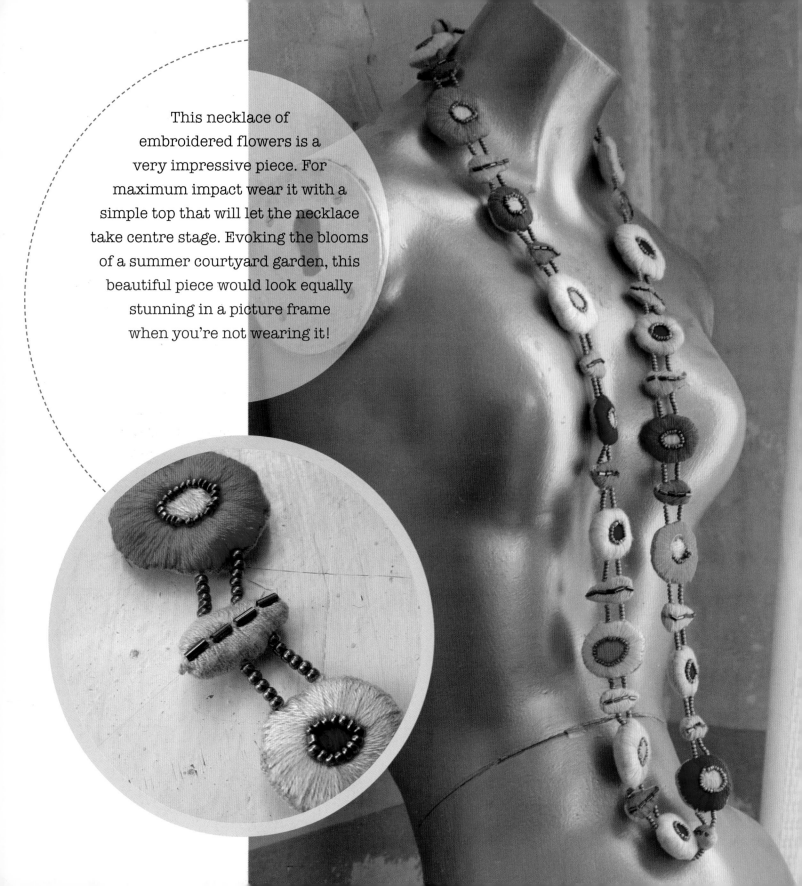

This necklace of embroidered flowers is a very impressive piece. For maximum impact wear it with a simple top that will let the necklace take centre stage. Evoking the blooms of a summer courtyard garden, this beautiful piece would look equally stunning in a picture frame when you're not wearing it!

embroidered necklace

Flowers and leaves

For each embroidered flower cut out circles from the base fabric with the following diameters:

Large flowers: two 5cm/2in (A) and four 4cm/1¾in (B). Cut out enough for seven large flowers. Small flowers: two 4cm/1¾in (C) and four 3cm/1⅛in (D). Cut out enough for 10 small flowers.

For each leaf cut: two 1.5cm/⅝in (E) long leaf shapes and four 1cm/⅜in (F) long leaf shapes. Cut out enough for 18 leaves.

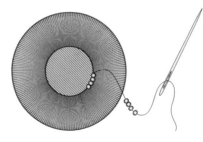

1 To make a large flower base, fold under the edges of each piece A. Sandwich four pieces of B between two of A, and whipstitch together. Repeat to make seven bases. Repeat with the small flower shapes, sandwiching four pieces of D between two of C, to make 10 flowers. Make 18 leaves in the same way. Embroider the flower base. Using a fabric marker pen, draw a circle 1.5cm (⅝in) in diameter in the centre of the base. Work satin stitch across the centre (see page 107). Work satin stitches in stranded embroidery thread around the edge in a contrasting colour for the petals.

2 Thread four bronze seed beads onto a length of No. 8 embroidery thread and attach them around the centre of the flower. Repeat until you have completed the circle. Repeat to add beads to the centre of all the flowers.

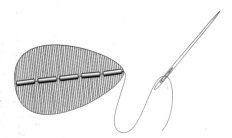

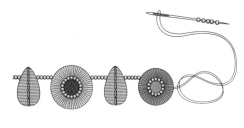

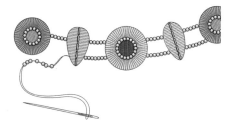

3 To complete the leaf, work straight stitches or satin stitch in stranded embroidery thread across the leaf, separating the right and the left at the centre of the leaf. Attach four or five bugle beads down the centre of the leaf.

4 Join the flowers together in the following sequence: leaf, large flower, leaf, small flower. To join the flowers, thread a needle with No. 8 embroidery thread, string on approximately five small round beads, knot the thread, then take the needle through the leaf base and out on the opposite side. Tie a knot, then thread on five beads, knot the thread and attach a flower in the same way.

5 After the last leaf, make a ring clasp at the end of the inside loop (see page 106). Then add the outer necklace loop, adding six or seven beads between each flower and leaf to adjust the length of the loop.

Flowers and leaves

For each embroidered flower cut out circles from the base fabric with the following diameters: two 5cm/2in (A) and four 4cm/1¾in (B). Cut out enough for 10 flowers. Make each flower base following the instructions in Step 1 on page 21. Embroider each flower with contrasting threads and attach small bronze beads to the centre, following the instructions in Step 2 on page 21. To make the leaf clasp, cut out two 1.5cm/⅝in long leaf shapes and four 1cm/½in long leaf shapes. Make the leaf following the instructions in Step 3 on page 22.

Materials

- 1m (1yd) cotton fabric
- Fabric marker pen
- Embroidery needle
- Stranded embroidery thread in a selection of colours (fuchsia pink, pale pink, off-white, white, orange, light green)
- Bronze seed beads
- 6mm pink Czech cut beads
- 5mm green bugle beads

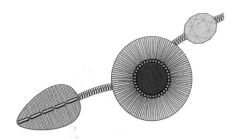

1 Attach the leaf to the flowers with a length of chain crochet (page 111), then join the flowers together with a loop of chain crochet, incorporating a Czech bead between each flower.

2 After the last flower, add a bead and make the end of the inside loop part of the ring clasp (see page 106). Add the outer necklace loop, adding beads between each flower and adding more chain stitches between the beads to adjust the length, if necessary.

The perfect complement to the long double-strand necklace, or fantastic on its own, this pretty bracelet combines a simple palette of colours with delicate pink faceted beads. This piece would be perfect with a floaty summer dress at cocktail hour.

Bring a tired handbag back to life with this stylish flower charm or key ring in soft yarns and vibrant colours. It can easily be adapted to hang from a belt loop, your mobile phone or even your dog's lead! Small and simple, it is a wonderful piece to make and give to your friends.

variation:

embroidered *key ring*

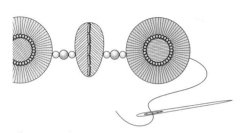

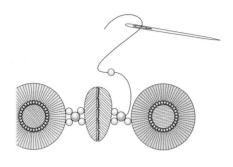

Materials

• 1m (1yd) cotton fabric
• Fabric marker pen
• Embroidery needle
• Stranded embroidery thread
  in a selection of colours
  (fuchsia pink, pale pink,
  taupe, orange, light green)
• Bronze seed beads
• Faceted beads
• Small round beads
• Large round beads
• Two 8mm jump rings

Make a base for each embroidered flower (three large and two small, see page 24), then embroider and embellish with beads (see Steps 1–2, page 21). Make four leaf shapes following Step 3 on page 22. Thread a needle and string on a faceted bead. Bring the needle out through the first flower, string on a small bead, a large bead and a small bead, then join through the centre of a leaf, bringing the needle out on the opposite side and stringing on beads in the same order. Join the flowers and leaves, attaching a faceted bead on the end of the last flower.

2 String the outer loop, adding a small bead, passing the needle through the large bead and stringing another small bead between the flower and leaf.

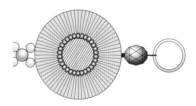

3 Bring the thread through the faceted bead and attach a jump ring to each end by threading on the jump ring, bringing the needle back through the bead and knotting to secure. Attach a clasp or key ring to the jump rings.

pompom *bracelet*

Materials
- DK yarn in several colours
- 3mm crochet hook
- Metal bracelet, 7cm (2¾in) in diameter
- Needle and beading thread
- Bronze seed beads

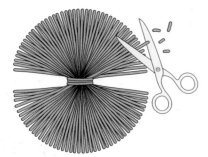

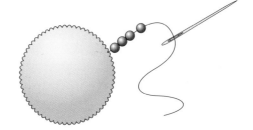

1 Make seven pompoms with a diameter of approximately 2.5cm (1in), in different coloured yarns (see page 104). Tie yarn to bracelet. Work dc over bracelet until it is covered. Fasten off. Sew in ends, joining first dc to last dc.

2 Thread a needle with beading thread and push it through the centre of a pompom. Thread on four or five seed beads.

3 Take the needle through the edge of the crochet and sew it in place with a double knot, then take the thread back through the beads and secure the thread in the pompom. Attach the remaining six pompoms equidistantly around the bracelet. Make several bracelets in different colours to wear together.

This fun pompom bracelet brings to mind a circus costume or a folk tambourine. I love to wear several bracelets together, with a gradation of colours from yellow to orange, pink to purple, green to blue, and pale grey to dark grey. A single bracelet with multicoloured pompoms looks modern and striking. However you use them, making the downy pompoms is an enjoyable job.

Give your cherished
but worn cashmere sweaters a
new life as beautiful flowers. All your
fond memories associated with the
sweaters are in the flowers, which can be
looped around your waist as a single-strand
belt, or wrapped around your neck to keep
you warm. I find making cashmere flowers
very enjoyable work – it's a little like
baking cookies using similar techniques
to making dough, with an equally
sweet end result!

cashmere flowers

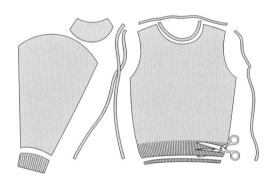

1 Wash your cashmere sweaters gently – don't worry if they shrink a little. Cut a sweater into its component parts – body, sleeves, hems and cuffs. Cut strips along the edges. The ribs of hems and cuffs are stretchy and work well as the centre of the flowers (A).

Cut strips to the following widths:

Rolled flowers:

Centre of flower (A): 1.5cm (⅝in) wide

Rolled petals (B): 2cm (¾in) wide

Eight-petalled flowers:

Centre of flower (C): 1.5cm (⅝in) wide

Petals (D): 8mm (⅜in) wide

techniques: *rolled* flowers

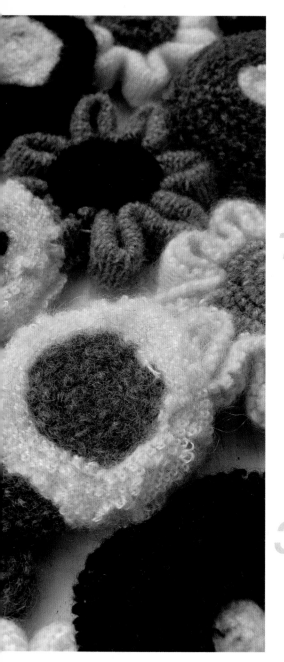

Making rolled flowers

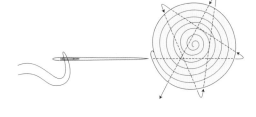

1 Roll a strip of Cord A until it measures 1.5cm (¾in) in diameter. Thread a needle with a double length of elastic yarn and push it through the centre of the roll to secure the end. Trim the excess strip.

2 To hold the roll in place, push the needle through in a zigzag pattern, ensuring the threads are pulled taut. The centre of the flower is complete.

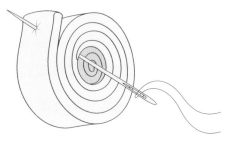

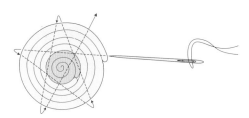

3 Roll a strip of Cord B around the centre of the flower until the flower measures 4cm (1⅛in) in diameter. Trim the excess strip. Push the needle through from the inside of the roll and secure the end of Cord B.

4 Push the needle through the whole flower in a zigzag pattern as in Step 2, ensuring that the shape of the roll remains round and smooth.

eight-petalled flowers

Making eight-petalled flowers

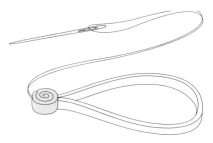

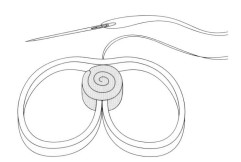

1 Repeat Steps 1–2 opposite to make the flower centre using C. Cut a 23-cm (9-in) length of D and fold it in half lengthways, right sides together. Push the needle through the centre of the end of the strip and the centre of the roll, drawing the thread through.

2 Take the needle through the end of the loop of cord D and pull the thread through, drawing the cord against the centre.

3 Take the needle in next to the cord and bring it out on the side opposite a loop in the cord. Pull to tauten. Push the needle through the side of the roll.

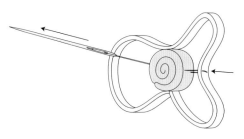

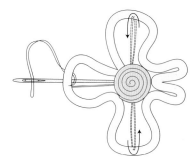

4 Take the needle through from the outside of the cord and back into the centre next to the thread, bringing it out on the opposite side diagonally. Pull to tauten, forming a second petal. Repeat to make four petals.

5 Repeat Steps 3–4 to make four more of these petals.

6 Knot the thread to complete the flower. Continue to make the required number of flowers for your project.

Once you have made your flowers it is very simple to attach them together to create a cosy scarf that will brighten any winter coat or jacket.

double *scarf*

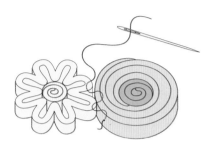

Materials
- Embroidery needle
- Elastic yarn No. 30 (thick)
- Old cashmere sweaters, in a selection of different colours
- 28 rolled flowers (see page 32)
- 28 eight-petalled flowers (see page 33)

1 Thread a needle and push it through the edge of a rolled flower and a petal of an eight-petalled flower and back to the rolled flower to join them. Take the needle out again opposite the adjacent petal and attach together.

2 Take the needle through the rolled flower and join an eight-petalled flower on the opposite side in the same way. Continue to join alternate petalled flowers and rolled flowers to form a row of 28 flowers. Knot the thread on the last flower to secure.

3 Repeat Steps 1–2 to make another strip of 28 flowers, then join the two strips together. Alternatively, you can join the double row together as you work.

Variation: Single scarf
You can wear this as a scarf, or alternatively as a belt around jeans or a knit dress.

1 Make 24 eight-petalled flowers and 24 rolled flowers. Attach alternate flowers together as above. In order to keep the petals open, sew to the rolled flower from the inside edge of the petal. Knot the thread on the last flower to secure.

variation:
cashmere flower *bracelet*

1 Thread a needle with stretch waxed thread. Push the needle through the upper portion of a flower, approximately 1cm (½in) from the top, and then through a roll at the same place. Repeat to join four flowers and four rolls alternately. Knot the thread to secure.

2 Push the needle though the lower portion of the flower approximately 1cm (½in) from the base and attach it to a rolled flower. Continue to join the flowers together. Knot the thread to secure at the end.

3 To complete the bracelet, tie the thread ends together with a knot.

With elasticated thread, this fits snugly to your wrist and is very comfortable and cosy on a chilly day. Match the colours to your winter coat, or a favourite woolly cardigan, and you will be ready to face any weather in style.

This long necklace is
very easy to string together
and you can adjust the length by
simply adding or reducing the
number of flowers. The wonderful
texture of the woolly textiles brings
warmth to any outfit. Don't feel that
you have to wear this in the
conventional way – tied loosely
around your waist, it looks
great as a belt, too!

variation:
mini cashmere flower *necklace*

Make 39 small petalled flowers (see page 33), using Cord A: 8mm x 6cm (⅜in x 2¼in), Cord B: 1.8mm x 13.5cm (¹⁄₁₆in x 5¼in). Create flowers in three colourways.

Materials

- Embroidery needle
- Elastic yarn No. 30 (thick)
- Old cashmere sweaters, in a selection of different colours
- Pearl cotton embroidery thread No. 8, red or to tone with the sweaters

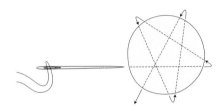

1 Make a ball using a strip of wool 1cm x 7cm (½in x 2¾in). Stitch through the ball in a zigzag to maintain its shape. Make a ring clasp with two or three loops of yarn with a diameter slightly larger than the ball (see page 106).

2 Thread a needle with double embroidery thread. Push the needle through the base of the ring clasp and tie the thread in a double knot. Push the needle through a petal and the centre of the flower and make a knot in the thread.

3 Take the needle out through a petal and attach the next flower following the instructions in Step 2, leaving a length of approximately 1.5cm (⅝in) between each flower.

4 Attach the ball to the last flower, securing with a double knot and leaving a 5mm (¼in) length of thread between the flower and the ball.

linen flower necklace

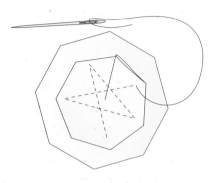

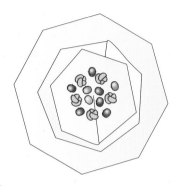

Materials

- ½m (½yd) linen
- Embroidery needle
- Pearl cotton embroidery thread No. 8, beige
- Multicoloured seed beads
- Delica beads

1 Copy the templates on pages 120–121 to make card templates and cut out 12 pieces of each hexagonal shape in linen and four pieces of the leaf shape. Place B on A. Make a tuck across the centre of B and tack to A with random stitches. Repeat to make 11 more petals.

2 Place C on B, make a tuck and attach to the two layers with small stitches. Embroider five French knots (see page 107) randomly in the centre of a flower. Embroider some seeds beads around them. Make 11 more flowers.

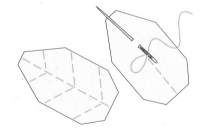

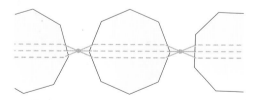

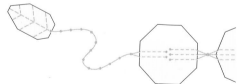

3 Sew two leaf shapes together (right) and embroider running stitches to represent the leaf veins (left).

4 Join the flowers together using triple running stitches on the reverse of the larger petal (A) only, making a knot between flowers. Be careful not to sew onto the top two layers, avoiding the stitches showing through.

5 Stop the stitches and make a knot to secure at the centre of the last flower. Sew double running stitches from the centre to the edge of the last flower. Bring the two threads together and make knots at 1.5cm (⅝in) intervals along a 17cm (6½in) length. Join the end leaf to the threads. Repeat to attach the leaf at the other end.

The frayed edges of the flowers make a fashionable accent in this statement necklace – you won't need any other accessories. Try different colourways: black linen with multicoloured beads is dramatic and strong, and with black beads is chic; white linen with multicoloured beads looks cute, and with white beads is very elegant. You can easily extend the pattern to make an unusual belt, too.

A linen flower hair accessory is a useful piece to complement your necklace; you could also attach it to a brooch pin for an informal corsage.

variation:
linen flower *hair clip*

Materials
- Linen
- Embroidery needle
- Pearl cotton embroidery thread No. 8, beige
- Multicoloured seed beads
- Delica beads
- Barrette or brooch pin

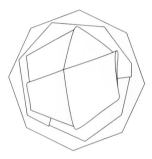

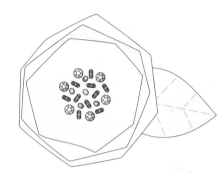

1 Copy the templates on pages 118–119 and make card templates. Cut out two pieces of the hexagonal and leaf shapes from fabric. Place B on A and make two tucks in B. Place C on B and make four tucks in C. Pin in place.

2 Thread double embroidery yarn through the needle and layer the two leaf shapes, sewing leaf veins in place following the instructions in Step 3 on page 40. Sew the petals and leaf together on the reverse, taking care not to show the stitches on the upper side. Hide the stitches inside tucks on petal C. Work 10 French knots (see page 107) and attach seed beads in the centre of the flower. Sew larger beads around them. Attach a barrette or brooch pin to the back.

vibrant beaded *collar*

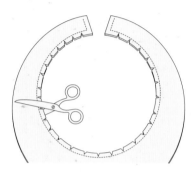

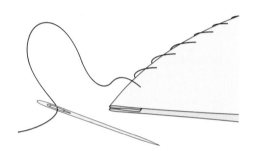

Materials

- 15-cm (6-in) square quilted beige linen
- 15-cm (6-in) square beige linen for lining
- Pearl cotton embroidery thread No. 8, to match
- Selection of beads, such as seed beads, large cut beads, round beads, flat beads

1 Copy the template on page 117 and cut out two necklace base shapes from the quilted linen and the lining. Place right sides together and sew a 5mm (¼in) seam across the ends and around the inner circle. Carefully snip into the curve to ease the seam.

2 Turn right sides out and press the stitched seam carefully to form a smooth curve. Turn under the outer edge to the wrong side by 1cm (½in) on the top and base. Press, then hand stitch together and press again.

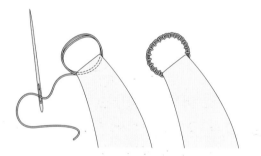

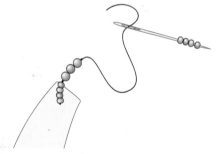

3 Thread a needle with embroidery thread and make a ring clasp (see page 106) along the end of one side.

4 Make the catch on the opposite edge. Thread a needle and bring it out about 2cm (¾in) inside from the edge and work a French knot (see page 107). Thread four seed beads onto the thread and make a knot. Thread on three round beads, make a knot and thread four seed beads. Sew a few stitches and make a knot to secure, then cut off the thread.

Made from a heavy linen, this luxurious collar, embellished with an array of sparkling beads, will bring instant glamour to any outfit. Perfect for evening wear, it will also look impressive against a plain-knit sweater and jeans.

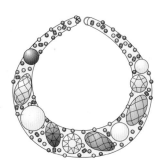

5 Attach beads to the base, taking care not to show the stitches on the reverse. Sew the larger stones in place first, then the smaller stones and add a few French knots or bullion knots, or other decorative stitches.

6 Attach the beads to the edge, starting with the central bead in the middle of the necklace and then adding a bead alternately on the left and right, judging the distance between the beads by eye. Bringing the needle out from the back of the hem at the base, thread on two round beads, a teardrop bead and a round bead. Bring the thread back through the teardrop bead and a round bead, sew a knot at the hem to secure. Bring the needle out approximately 2.5cm (1in) along to attach the next bead. Repeat to attach 11 hanging beads in total.

Variation: Muted beaded collar
With an understated colour palette, this collar looks cool and chic.

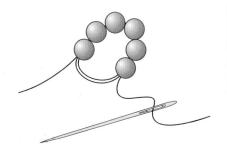

1 Repeat Steps 1–3 on page 44. Make a catch as a part of clasp on the other side of the bases. Bring the needle out about 2cm (¾in) inside from the edge and work a French knot. Thread six round beads and bring the thread through the beads twice before making a knot and securing. Embellish the necklace base shape with your chosen design (see Steps 4–5 above).

Materials
- 15-cm (6-in) square quilted beige linen
- 15-cm (6-in) square beige linen for lining
- Pearl cotton embroidery thread No. 8, to match
- Selection of beads, such as large cut beads, round beads, flat beads, teardrop beads

These projects use a few
basic crochet stitches to create
some beautifully-textured pieces
of jewellery. From simple, embellished
rings to the delicate cascade of flowers fit for
a bride, there are projects to suit all levels
of ability. Using wool, silk, cotton and
raffia, the variations are endless and you
will soon find many other uses
for the flowers, chains and
crosses that you create.

crocheted pieces

raffia bead necklace

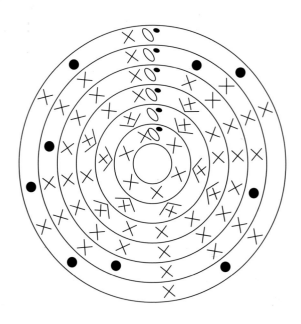

1 Large beads:

Make 2ch.

Round 1 1 6dc in second ch from hook, ss in 1ch.

Round 2 1ch, 2dc in each dc, ss in 1ch. 12dc.

Round 3 1ch, 1dc in first dc, [1dc in next dc, 2dc in next dc] twice, 1dc in each of next 3dc, 2dc in next dc, 1dc in each of next 2dc, 2dc in last dc, ss in 1ch. 16dc.

Round 4 1ch, 1dc in each dc, ss in 1ch.

Round 5 1ch, [1dc in each of 3dc, miss 1dc] 4 times, ss in 1ch. 12dc.

Round 6 1ch, [1dc in dc, miss 1dc] 6 times, ss in 1ch. 6dc.

Cut yarn, thread end through front loop of each dc, pull tight to close hole. Fasten off securely.

Make 16 large beads in assorted shades.

This simple necklace makes a bold accent on T-shirts or a linen dress in summer with the strong colours of the raffia yarns glowing in the sunshine. A flower clasp is a very charming part of the necklace – you can enjoy it at the front or the back.

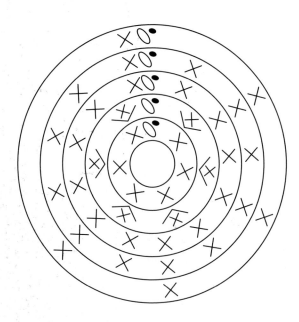

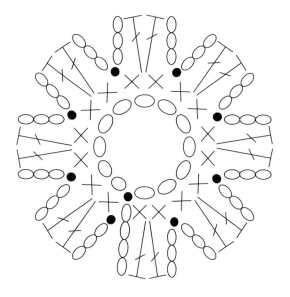

2 Bead clasp:

Make 2ch.

Round 1 6dc in second ch from hook, ss in 1ch.

Round 2 1ch, 2dc in each dc, ss in 1ch. 12dc.

Round 3 1ch, 1dc in each dc, ss in 1ch.

Round 4 1ch, 1dc in each dc, ss in 1ch.

Round 5 1ch, [1dc in dc, miss 1dc] 6 times, ss in 1ch. 6dc.

Cut yarn, thread end through front loop of each dc, pull tight to close hole. Fasten off securely.

3 Flower clasp:

Make 12ch, ss in first ch to form a ring.

Round 1 1ch, 16dc in ring, ss in first ch.

Round 2 [3ch, 2tr in next dc, 3ch, ss in next dc] 8 times, ss in first ch.

Fasten off.

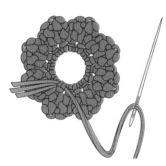

4 Thread a tapestry needle with a 1m (1¼yd) length of yarn and secure through a stitch on the reverse of the flower clasp.

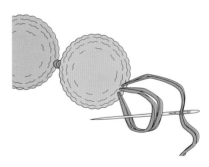

5 Push the needle through the centre of a large bead and knot to secure. Alternating colours, continue until all beads are joined, ending with bead clasp. Push needle back through bead clasp and fasten off securely. Push bead clasp through hole in centre of flower clasp to fasten necklace.

glasses cord

 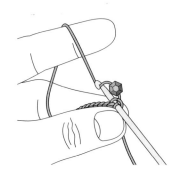

Materials
- Pearl cotton embroidery thread No. 8
- 24 x 5mm faceted beads
- 2mm crochet hook
- Two spectacle holders
- Two front-opening calottes
- Two jump rings
- Jewellery pliers

1 Thread a 4.5m (5yd) length of cotton embroidery thread through the needle, then thread 24 beads onto the yarn. Remove the needle.

2 Make five chains in the thread, slip one bead close to the hook, yarn over and pull through the loop on the hook.

3 Continue to make chains, slipping a bead in each seventh chain, finishing with five chains after the final bead. Fasten off. Cut both ends of the yarn to leave tails of 3cm (1¼in).

4 To attach the end fastenings, thread one tail of thread through a front-opening calotte and knot to secure. Close the calotte using jewellery pliers, attach a jump ring, then attach a speactacle holder to the jump ring. Close the jump ring. Repeat for the other end.

A beautiful glasses cord is the perfect accessory if you wear spectacles, and makes a great addition to sunglasses, too. These light, stylish cords are embellished with faceted beads – they are so simple to make that you can soon produce a range of colours to match your favourite outfits. You'll be instantly transformed into a powerful CEO or a devilish fashion editor – but never a granny!

The inspiration for these designs came from the cowgirls of the Wild West. I like to wear three bracelets together, in different colours – perfect with jeans or a simple knit dress. Your choice of yarn is important – a cotton yarn is light and summery; a wool yarn is warm and rich, perfect for accessorizing autumn and winter knits. While they look fantastic together, each piece makes a bold statement on its own – just remember to wear them with a fringed suede skirt and boots!

tassel bracelet

1 Make seven 4cm (1½in) tassels in different coloured yarns with contrasting bands (see page 105). Thread a needle with beading thread and attach to tassel above contrasting band. Thread on enough beads to fit around tassel and join to form a ring. Take needle under contrasting band and work another ring of beads. Fasten off securely.

Materials

- DK yarn in a selection of colours
- 3mm crochet hook
- Metal bracelet
- Length of clear nylon beading thread
- Bronze seed beads

Key:

ss (slip stitch)	●
ch (chain stitch)	○
dc (double crochet)	✕

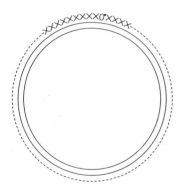

2 Tie yarn to bracelet. Work dc over bracelet until it is covered. Fasten off. Sew in ends, joining first dc to last dc.

3 Thread a needle with beading thread, attach to the bracelet and thread on five small beads. Push the needle through the top of a tassel, bring the thread back through the beads and secure neatly to the bracelet. Attach the remaining six tassels equidistantly around the bracelet. Make two more bracelets, either in matching or contrasting colours, and wear together or separately.

variations:

tassel *ring*

This five-tassel ring is a star in its own right – be bold!

Key:

ss (slip stitch)	•
ch (chain stitch)	o
dc (double crochet)	×

Materials

- DK yarn in a selection of colours
- 3mm crochet hook
- Length of clear nylon beading thread
- Selection of bronze seed beads
- Gold metallic yarn
- Needle

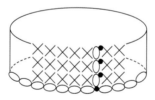

1 Make five beaded tassels in different coloured yarns (see page 105). With metallic yarn make 20ch, ss in first ch to form a ring. Number of ch can be adjusted to fit finger.

Round 1 1ch, 1dc in each ch, ss in 1ch.
Round 2 1ch, 1dc in each dc, ss in 1ch.
Round 3 As round 2.
Fasten off.

2 Thread the needle with the beading thread and attach to the ring. Thread on five beads, then push the needle through the top of a tassel and bring the thread back through the beads. Secure and cut the thread. Attach four more tassels to the centre of the ring in the same way.

tassel *necklace*

You can adjust the length of the necklace with the ribbon tie. This design can easily be extended to make a fabulous belt.

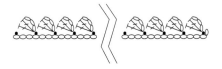

1 Make eleven 5.5–6cm (2¼in) beaded tassels in different coloured yarns (see page 105). Make 65ch.
Row 1 Ss in 2nd ch [3ch, 2tr in same place as ss, miss 2ch, ss in the next ch] to end. Fasten off.

Key:

ss (slip stitch)	•
ch (chain stitch)	O
tr (treble crochet)	T

Materials

- DK yarn in a selection of colours
- 3mm crochet hook
- Length of clear nylon beading thread
- Selection of bronze seed beads
- Czech cut beads
- 1.6m (1¾yd) suede ribbon

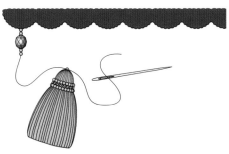

2 Thread the needle with the beading thread and attach to the edge of a crochet scallop. Thread on two seed beads, one Czech cut bead and two seed beads. Push the needle through the top of a tassel and bring the thread back through the beads. Secure the thread to the top of scallop. Attach a tassel on alternate scallops.

3 Cut ribbon into two equal lengths. Fold one length in half and knot folded end through end of necklace. Repeat with other length.

crocheted disks necklace

1 Bead:

Round 1 Wrap yarn around finger to form a ring, 3ch, 11tr in ring, ss in top of 3ch.
Round 2 1ch, 1dc in same place as ss, [2dc in next tr, 1dc in next tr] 5 times, 2dc in last tr, ss in 1ch.
Fasten off. Make a total of 28 beads.

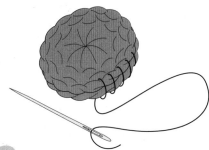

2 With wrong sides together, sew beads together in pairs joining through stitches of round 2.
Make 14 double beads.

3 Clasp ring:

Make 12ch, ss in first ch to form a ring.
Round 1 1ch, 12dc in ring, ss in 1ch.
Fasten off.

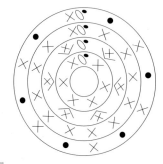

4 Clasp ball:

Round 1 Wrap yarn around finger to form a ring, 1ch, 6dc in ring, ss in 1ch.
Round 2 1ch, 2dc in each dc, ss in 1ch, 12dc.
Round 3 1ch, 1dc in each dc, ss in 1ch.
Round 4 1ch, [1dc in next dc, miss next dc] 6 times, ss in 1ch.
Fasten off.

Materials

- Pearl cotton embroidery thread No. 5, red
- 2mm crochet hook
- Embroidery needle
- 15 cut coral beads

Key:

ss (slip stitch)	●
ch (chain stitch)	o
dc (double crochet)	×
tr (treble crochet)	†
2dc in same st	⋎

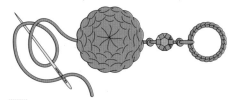

5 Thread a needle with embroidery thread and secure end to clasp ring.
*Make a knot, thread on a coral bead, make a knot, thread on a double bead pushing needle from edge to edge through centre of double bead, repeat from * until all double beads are threaded, make a knot, thread on a coral bead, make a knot and attach clasp ball. Fasten off securely.

Some islands in the
world are surrounded by pink
coral and so have pink beaches –
sunset must be so romantic there.
I used genuine pink coral beads for this
necklace, imagining it would transport
me to a southern island, with the
waves breaking on the pink sand.
This piece would look great with a
vintage lace blouse or dress, but I
also like to wear it with just a
simple shirt.

Cherries bring back
happy childhood memories
of baskets full of the sweet
fruit, in beautiful tones of reds and
pinks. I wanted to capture these
memories in a necklace so that I could
enjoy this wonderful fruit even
out of season! You can vary the
colours with deep red, pink
and light green cherries.

cherry necklace

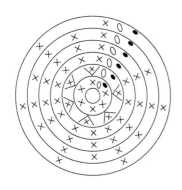

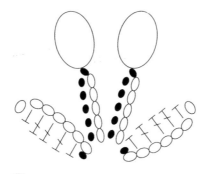

1 Cherry:

Using red, wrap yarn around finger to form a ring.

Round 1 1ch, 6dc in ring, ss in first ch. Pull up end to tighten ring.

Round 2 1ch, 2dc in each dc, ss in first ch. 12dc.

Round 3 1ch, 1dc in each dc, ss in first ch.

Rounds 4 and 5 As round 3.

Round 6 1ch, [1dc in next dc, miss next dc] 6 times. 6dc.

Fasten off leaving a 15cm (6in) length of yarn.

Thread end through front loop each of dc of round 6, draw up and fasten off securely.

Make a total of 24 cherries.

2 Leaves and stalks:

Using green, *make 7ch, miss first ch, 1htr in next ch, 1tr in each of next 3ch, 1htr in next ch, ss in last ch** – first leaf completed, [5ch, ss in top of a cherry, 1ss in each of 5ch] twice, rep from * to ** – second leaf completed, ss in same place as 1st ss of first leaf***. Do not fasten off.

Materials
- 3mm crochet hook
- Pearl cotton embroidery thread No. 8 in red and green

Key:

ch (chain stitch)	o
ss (slip stitch)	•
dc (double crochet)	×
htr (half treble)	⊤
tr (treble crochet)	⨍
2dc in same st	⤬

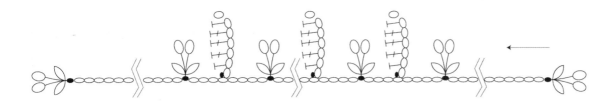

Make 60ch, [work from * to ***, make
4ch, work from * to ** for a single leaf,
make 4ch] 9 times, work from * to ***,
make 60ch, work from * to ***.
Fasten off.
Tie ends of necklace in bow.

variation:

cherry *bracelet*

This bracelet looks sweet accompanying the necklace on the previous page, but is equally effective on its own. Try crocheting it in mixed berry tones, too. You could even make a pair of matching earrings.

Materials

• 3mm crochet hook
• Pearl cotton embroidery thread No. 8, red and green

Key:

ch (chain stitch)	O
ss (slip stitch)	●
dc (double crochet)	✕
htr (half treble)	T
tr (treble)	⊤

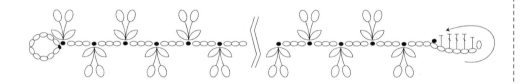

1 Using red, make 28 cherries (see Step 1, page 63).

Using green, make a single leaf (for fastener), *make 3ch, work first leaf, [work stalk and join a cherry] twice, work second leaf (see Step 2, page 63), rep from* 13 times, make 10ch, ss in 1st of 10ch (for fastening ring). Fasten off.

flower *corsage*

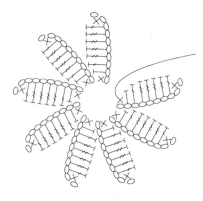

1 Petals:

Using pink, *make 10ch, 1dc in 2nd ch
from hook. 1tr in next ch, 1dtr in each of
next 4ch, 1tr in next ch, 1htr in next ch,
1dc in last ch, rep from * until a total of
8 petals have been worked.
Fasten off leaving a 60cm (24in) length
of yarn.

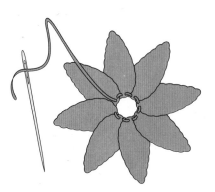

2
With WS facing arrange petals to form a
circle, overlapping petals. Catch ends tog
at centre.

Materials
- 4mm crochet hook
- Rayon raffia yarn in pink,
  yellow and green
- Brooch pin

Key:

ss (slip stitch)	●
ch (chain stitch)	0
dc (double crochet)	×
htr (half treble)	T
tr (treble)	Ŧ
dtr (double treble)	Ŧ

This raffia corsage will add an accent of casual elegance to your wardrobe. A corsage is extremely versatile and shouldn't be worn only on special occasions – the sharp, modern lines of the petals bring a casual elegance to an everyday shirt. Try wearing several corsages together for a colourful bouquet effect!

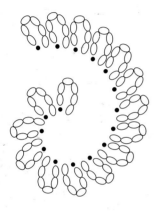

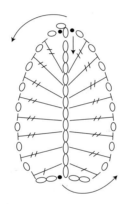

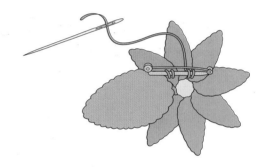

3 Flower centre:

Using yellow, *make 6ch, ss in first of 6ch, rep from * until there are 16 loops. Fasten off leaving a 20cm (8in) length of yarn.

Wind the length of loops round to form the centre and sew tog on WS.

4 Leaf:

Using green, make 15ch, 1tr in 4th ch from hook, [1ch, 1dtr in next ch] 7 times, 1ch, miss 3ch, 1ss, 1ch and 1ss in last ch, working along other side of ch work 1ch, miss 3ch, [1dtr in next ch, 1ch] 7 times, 1tr in next ch, 2ch, ss in next ch. Fasten off.

5

Place flower centre in middle of petals and sew securely on WS. Sew end of leaf to WS of flower. Sew brooch pin to WS of flower.

In warm, toning colours, this corsage would also look lovely pinned to the ribbon of a summer straw hat or adding a touch of glamour to an everyday shopping basket. Experiment with colour combinations to see you through the seasons.

variation:
12-petalled flower *corsage*

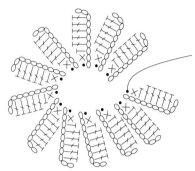

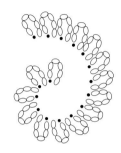

Materials

- 4mm crochet hook
- Rayon raffia yarn, off-white, beige, brown
- Brooch pin

Key:

ss (slip stitch)	●
ch (chain stitch)	○
dc (double crochet)	×
htr (half treble)	T
tr (treble)	₸
dtr (double treble)	₸

1 Petals:

Using off white, *make 10ch, miss 2ch, 1tr in each of next 5ch, 1htr in next ch, 1dc in next ch, 1ss in last ch, rep from * until a total of 12 petals have been worked. Fasten off leaving a 60cm (24in) length of yarn.

With WS facing arrange petals to form a circle, overlapping petals. Catch ends tog at centre (see Step 2, page 66).

2 Flower centre:

Using beige, *make 6ch, ss in first of 6ch, rep from * until there are 16 loops. Fasten off leaving a 20cm (8in) length of yarn.

Wind the length of loops round to form the centre and sew tog on WS.

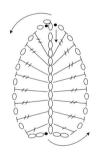

3 Leaf:

Using brown, make 15ch, 1tr in 4th ch from hook, [1ch, 1dtr in next ch] 7 times, 1ch, miss 3ch, 1ss, 1ch and 1ss in last ch, working along other side of ch work 1ch, miss 3ch, [1dtr in next ch, 1ch] 7 times, 1tr in next ch, 2ch, ss in next ch.

Fasten off. Make a second leaf. Place flower centre in middle of petals and sew securely on WS. Sew end of leaves to WS of flower. Sew brooch pin to WS of flower (see Step 5, page 68).

cross necklace

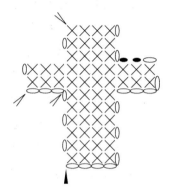

Materials
- 3mm crochet hook
- Fine Rayon raffia yarn, off-white

Key:

ss (slip stitch)   •

ch (chain stitch)   0

dc (double crochet)   ×

1 Cross:

Make 5ch.

Row 1 (RS)1dc in 2nd ch from hook, 1dc in each ch. 4dc.

Rows 2–6 1ch, 1dc in each of 4dc.

Join a short length of yarn to 1ch at start of row 6 and make 3ch. Fasten off.

Row 7 4ch, 1dc in 2nd ch from hook, 1dc in each of next 2ch, 1dc in each of next 4dc, 1dc in each of 3ch. 10dc.

Row 8 1ch, 1dc in each of 10dc.

Row 9 1ch, miss 1st dc, 1ss in each of next 2dc, 1ch, 1dc in each of next 4dc, turn. 4dc.

Rows 10–11 1ch, 1dc in each of 4dc.

Fasten off.

Make a 2nd cross.

With wrong sides tog, sew the 2 crosses tog around outer edges.

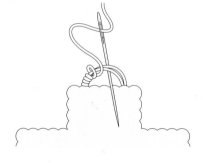

2 Sew a small loop at the centre of the top edge of the cross and cover the loop with whip stitch.

Made entirely from raffia yarn, this necklace and bracelet were inspired by an illustration from an antique book. The key to the success of the piece is the shape of the cross – it may take a little practice to get it right, but be patient and you will be rewarded.

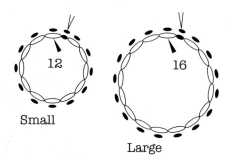

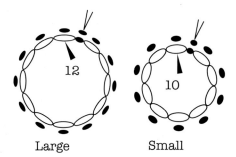

Small Large Large Small

Chain 1

Chain 2

3 Chain 1:

Large ring: Make 16ch, ss in 1st ch to join ring, 1ss in each ch, ss in 1st ss. Fasten off.
Small ring: Make 12ch, thread end through large ring, ss in 1st ch to join ring, 1ss in each ch, ss in 1st ss. Fasten off.
Make and link a large ring to small ring.
*Make and link a small ring to last large ring.
Make and link a large ring to last small ring.
Rep from *, making and linking small and large rings alternately, until 23 large and 22 small rings are joined into a length.

4 Chain 2, used for joining the cross:

Large ring: Make 12ch, ss in 1st ch to join ring, 1ss in each ch, ss in 1st ss. Fasten off.
Small ring: Make 10ch, thread end through large ring, ss in 1st ch to join ring, 1ss in each ch, ss in 1st ss. Fasten off.
Make and link large and small rings alternately until 9 large and 8 small rings are joined into a length, linking final large ring to both the last small ring and the centre large ring on Chain 1.

5 Clasp:

Make 7ch, 1dc in 2nd ch from hook, 1dc in each ch. 6dc. Fasten off.
Sew a small loop at the centre of the top edge of the clasp and cover the loop with whip stitch (see Step 2, page 72).

6 At one end of chain 1, make and link 2 small (10ch) rings and 1 large (12ch) ring. At other end, make and link 2 small (10ch) rings, also linking the second ring through the loop in the clasp.

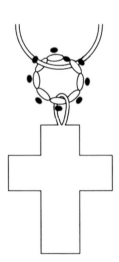

7 Make 8ch, thread end through large ring at end of chain 2 and through the loop on the cross, ss in 1st ch to join ring, 1ss in each ch, ss in 1st ss. Fasten off.

variation:

cross *choker*

For a touch of glamour, try making this in metallic threads and lamé yarns.

Materials
- 3mm crochet hook
- Fine Rayon raffia yarn, off-white

Key:

ss (slip stitch)	●
ch (chain stitch)	o
dc (double crochet)	×

1 *Cross:*

Make 3ch.

Row 1 (RS) 1dc in 2nd ch from hook, 1dc in next ch. 2dc.

Rows 2–6 1ch, 1dc in each of 2dc.

Join a short length of yarn to 1ch at start of row 6 and make 3ch. Fasten off.

Row 7 4ch, 1dc in 2nd ch from hook, 1dc in each of next

2ch, 1dc in each of next 2dc, 1dc in each of 3ch. 8dc.

Row 8 1ch, 1dc in each of 8dc.

Row 9 1ch, miss 1st dc, 1ss in each of next 2dc, 1ch, 1dc in each of next 2dc, turn. 2dc.

Rows 10–11 1ch, 1dc in each of 2dc.

Fasten off.

Make a total of 6 crosses.

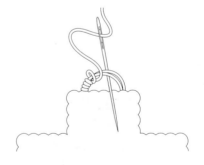

2 With wrong sides tog, join the crosses tog in pairs, sewing around outer edges to give 3 double crosses.

Sew a small loop at the centre of the top edge of each cross and cover the loop with whip stitch.

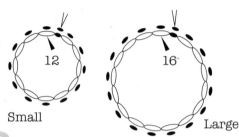

Small   Large

Chain:

Large ring Make 16ch, ss in 1st ch to join ring, 1ss in each ch, ss in 1st ss. Fasten off.

Small ring Make 12ch, thread end through large ring, ss in 1st ch to join ring, 1ss in each ch, ss in 1st ss. Fasten off. Make and link a large ring to small ring. *Make and link a small ring to last large ring. Make and link a large ring to last small ring. Rep from *, making and linking small and large rings alternately, until 10 large and 9 small rings are joined into a length.

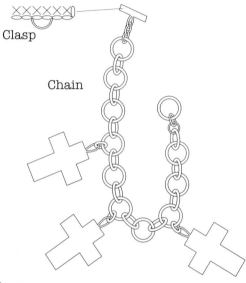

Clasp

Chain

Clasp:

Make 7ch, 1dc in 2nd ch from hook, 1dc in each ch. 6dc. Fasten off.

Sew a small loop at the centre of the top edge of the clasp and cover the loop with whip stitch (see Step 2, page 77).

At one end of chain, make and link 2 small (10ch) rings and 1 large (12ch) ring.

At other end, make and link 2 small (10ch) rings, also linking the second ring through the loop in the clasp.

Mark 3rd, 5th and 7th large rings of the chain.

Make 10ch, thread end through the loop on a cross then through one marked large ring, ss in 1st ch to join ring, 1ss in each ch, ss in 1st ss. Fasten off.

Attach the remaining 2 crosses in the same way.

silk flower ring

8-petalled silk flower

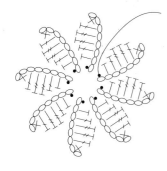

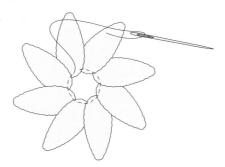

Materials
- 3mm crochet hook
- Silk yarn, off-white, beige
- Metallic yarn, gold
- Needle

Key:

ss (slip stitch)	•
ch (chain stitch)	o
dc (double crochet)	×
htr (half treble)	T
tr (treble crochet)	†
dtr (double treble)	‡

1 Petals:

Using off white, *make 8ch, 1dc in 2nd ch from hook. 1tr in next ch, 1dtr in each of next 2ch, 1tr in next ch, 1htr in next ch, 1ss in last ch, rep from * until a total of 8 petals have been worked.
Fasten off leaving a 30cm (12in) length of yarn.

2

With WS facing arrange petals to form a circle, overlapping petals. Catch ends tog at centre.

3 Flower centre:

Using beige, *make 6ch, ss in first of 6ch, rep from * until there are 10 loops. Fasten off leaving a 20cm (8in) length of yarn. Wind the length of loops round to form the centre and sew tog on WS.

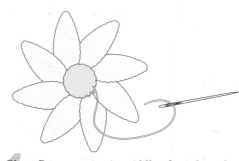

4

Place flower centre in middle of petals and sew securely on WS.

For these flower rings, I chose the same count of yarn but in a slightly darker colour for the centre so that the flowers are full of subtle ambiguities and look three-dimensional. The reflection of white silk makes your skin look smooth and bright, infusing it with the power of beauty.

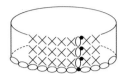

5 **Ring:**

Using metallic yarn, make 17ch, ss in first
ch to form a ring.

Number of ch can be adjusted to fit finger.

Round 1 1ch, 1dc in each ch, ss in 1ch.

Round 2 1ch, 1dc in each dc, ss in 1ch.

Round 3 As round 2.

Fasten off.

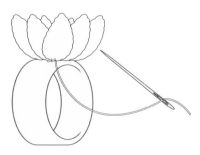

6 Place the flower on the ring covering the ss
in each round, and using off white sew
securely in place.

variation:
seven-petalled *silk flower*

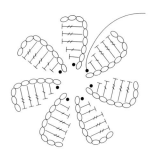

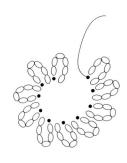

1 Petals:

Using beige, *make 9ch, miss 3ch, 1dtr in each of next 3ch, 1tr in next ch, 1htr in next ch, 1ss in last ch, rep from * until a total of 7 petals have been worked. Fasten off leaving a 30cm (12in) length of yarn. With WS facing arrange petals to form a circle, overlapping petals. Catch ends tog at centre.

2 Flower centre:

Using off white, *make 6ch, ss in first of 6ch, rep from * until there are 10 loops. Fasten off leaving a 20cm (8in) length of yarn. Wind the length of loops round to form the centre and sew tog on WS. Place flower centre in middle of petals and sew securely on WS.

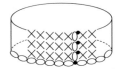

3 Ring:

Using metallic yarn, make 17ch, ss in first ch to form a ring.
Number of ch can be adjusted to fit finger.
Round 1 1ch, 1dc in each ch, ss in 1ch.
Round 2 1ch, 1dc in each dc, ss in 1ch.
Round 3 As round 2.

Fasten off.
Place the flower on the ring covering the ss in each round, and using beige sew securely in place.

These rings are
made of pink and green
cotton embroidery threads,
embellished with your
favourite beads in the centre.
Have fun choosing colours
from the huge range
available.

cotton flower ring

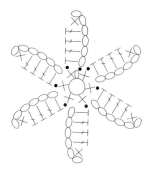

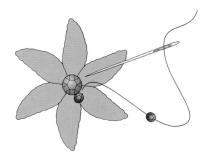

Materials

- 2.50mm crochet hook
- Pearl cotton embroidery thread No. 8, pink, beige
- One 6mm faceted bead
- Six 4mm faceted beads

Key:

ss (slip stitch)	●
ch (chain stitch)	O
dc (double crochet)	×
htr (half treble)	T
tr (treble crochet)	⊤

1 Petals:

Using pink, wrap yarn around finger to form a ring.

Round 1 1ch, 6dc in ring, ss in 1ch. Pull up end to tighten ring.

Round 2 [6ch, 1dc in 2nd ch from hook, 1tr in each of next 3ch, 1htr in last ch, 1ss in next dc of round 1] 6 times.

Fasten off leaving a 30cm (12in) length of yarn.

2 With WS facing, catch ends of petals tog, ensuring they meet at centre. With RS facing, sew 6mm bead in centre of flower, then sew six 4mm beads to form a ring around larger bead.

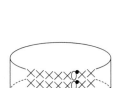

3 Ring:

Using beige, make 17ch, ss in first ch to form a ring.

Number of ch can be adjusted to fit finger.

Round 1 1ch, 1dc in each ch, ss in 1ch.

Round 2 1ch, 1dc in each dc, ss in 1ch.

Round 3 As round 2.

Fasten off.

Place the flower on the ring covering the ss in each round, and using pink sew securely in place.

variation:
eight-petalled *cotton flower*

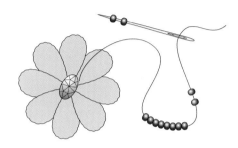

Materials
- 2.50mm crochet hook
- Pearl cotton embroidery thread No. 8, green, beige
- 6mm faceted bead
- Seed beads

Key:

ss (slip stitch)	●
ch (chain stitch)	O
dc (double crochet)	×
ttr (triple treble)	⊤

Petals:

1 Using green, wrap yarn around finger to form a ring.

Round 1 1ch, 8dc in ring, ss in 1ch. Pull up end to tighten ring.

Round 2 [4ch, 1ttr, 4ch, 1ss] in each dc of round 1, ss in first dc of round 1. Fasten off.

2 With WS facing, catch ends of petals tog, ensuring they meet at centre. With RS facing, sew 6mm bead in centre of flower, then sew seed beads in a circle around larger bead.

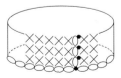

Ring:

3 Using beige, make 17ch, ss in first ch to form a ring.

Number of ch can be adjusted to fit finger.

Round 1 1ch, 1dc in each ch, ss in 1ch.

Round 2 1ch, 1dc in each dc, ss in 1ch.

Round 3 As round 2.

Fasten off.

Place the flower on the ring covering the ss in each round, and using green sew securely in place (see Step 6, page 82).

lamé *chain*

Materials

- 3mm crochet hook
- Metallic yarn in silver and gold

Key:

ss (slip stitch)	●
ch (chain stitch)	○
dc (double crochet)	×
tr (treble crochet)	†

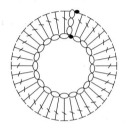

1 Rings:

Using silver yarn, make 20ch, ss in first
ch to form a ring.
Round 1 3ch, 35tr in ring, ss in top of 3ch.
Fasten off.
Make a total of 21 rings.

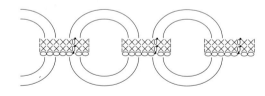

2 Links:

Using gold yarn, make 18ch.
With right side of rings facing, thread end
of ch through 2 rings taking care that it is
not twisted, ss in first ch to form a ring.
Round 1 1ch, 1dc in each ch, ss in 1ch.
Round 2 1ch, 1dc in each dc, ss in 1ch.
Fasten off.
Link all rings together in this way.

A big chain necklace of gold and silver lamé yarns is a very stylish piece which can be used on many occasions. The lightweight chain is easier to wear than its equivalent in metal and you can vary the length to suit your style, or make a longer one to wear as a belt, too.

I made this silk
necklace and bracelet for my
friend's wedding – she looked
very beautiful in a simple and
elegant dress with the swinging
flowers at her neck and wrist. Whether
you make it for yourself or a close
friend, sister or daughter, it will be a
heartfelt gift that will bring the
bride luck and happiness.

bridal flower necklace

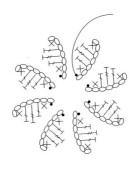

Flower A:

*Make 7ch, 1dc in 2nd ch from hook, 1tr in next ch, 1dtr in next ch, 1tr in next ch, 1dc in next ch, 1ss in last ch, rep from * until a total of 8 petals have been worked.

Fasten off leaving a 30cm (12in) length of yarn.

With WS facing arrange petals to form a circle, overlapping petals. Catch ends tog at centre.

Make a total of 16 of flower A.

Flower centre:

*Make 6ch, ss in first of 6ch, rep from * until there are 10 loops.

Fasten off leaving a 20cm (8in) length of yarn.

Wind the length of loops round to form the centre and sew tog on WS.

Make a total of 16 flower centres.

Sew a flower centre in middle of each flower A.

Materials
- 2.50mm crochet hook
- Medium-weight silk yarn, off-white

Key:

ss (slip stitch)	●
ch (chain stitch)	O
dc (double crochet)	×
tr (treble crochet)	⊤
dtr (double treble)	⊤

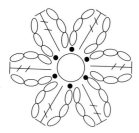

3 **Flower B:**
Wrap yarn around finger to form a ring.
Round 1 [3ch, 1dtr, 3ch, 1ss in ring] 6
times, ss in first ch.
Fasten off.
Pull up end to tighten ring.
Make a total of 8 of flower B.

4 **Leaf:**
Make 6ch.
Row 1 1dc in 2nd ch from hook, 1tr in
next ch, 1dtr in next ch, 1tr in next ch, ss
in last ch.
Fasten off.
Make a total of 51 leaves.

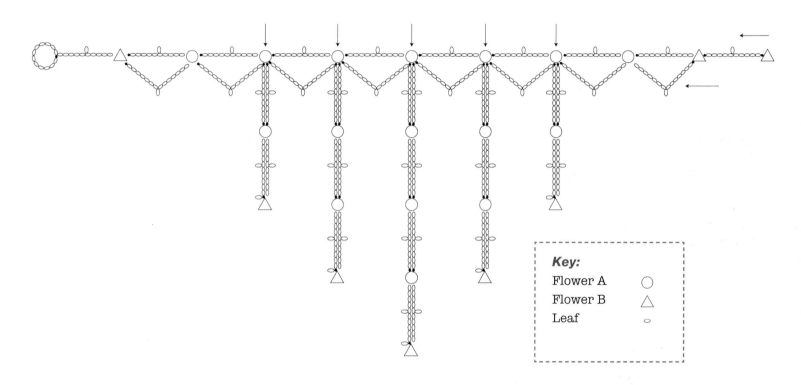

Key:

Flower A	◯
Flower B	△
Leaf	◦

5 Starting at top right of chart, link flowers and leaves tog with ch.

Top strand Join yarn to WS at centre of a flower B, 10ch, ss in a leaf, 6ch, ss in a flower B, [6ch, ss in leaf, 6ch, ss in flower A] 7 times, 6ch, ss in leaf, 6ch, ss in flower B, 6ch, ss in leaf, 16ch, ss in 10th ch to form fastening loop. Fasten off. This completes top strand of chart.

Second strand Starting at right of chart, join yarn to WS at centre of 2nd flower B of top strand, [7ch, ss in leaf, 7ch, ss in WS of flower A of top strand] 7 times, 7ch, ss in leaf, 7ch, ss in WS of flower B of top strand. Fasten off. This completes second strand of chart.

First drop Starting at right of chart, join yarn to WS at centre of 2nd flower A of top strand.

First side Working down from top strand, 5ch, ss in leaf, 5ch, ss in flower A, 5ch, ss in leaf, 5ch, ss in flower B.

Second side Working back towards top strand, [ss in leaf, 5ch] twice, ss in back of flower A of first side of drop, 5ch, ss in leaf, 5ch, ss in 2nd flower A on top strand. Fasten off.

This completes first drop.

Following chart, work remaining 4 drops.

variation:
bridal flower *bracelet*

These two pieces make a stunning set, but you could make them individually, in any colour to suit the occasion.

Materials
- 2.50mm crochet hook
- Medium-weight silk yarn, off-white

Key:

ss (slip stitch)	●
ch (chain stitch)	o
tr (treble crochet)	⊤
dtr (double treble)	⊥

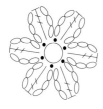

Flower A:

1 Wrap yarn around finger to form a ring.

Round 1 [3ch, 1dtr, 3ch, 1ss in ring] 6 times, ss in first ch.

Fasten off.

Pull up end to tighten ring.

Make a total of 11 of flower A.

Flower B:

2 Wrap yarn around finger to form a ring.

Round 1 [3ch, 1dtr, 3ch, 1ss in ring] 5 times, ss in first ch.

Fasten off.

Pull up end to tighten ring.

Make a total of 11 of flower B.

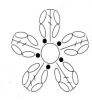

Flower fastener:

3 Wrap yarn around finger to form a ring.

Round 1 [2ch, 1tr, 2ch, 1ss in ring]
5 times, ss in first ch.

Fasten off.

Pull up end to tighten ring.

Make 1 flower fastener.

4 Starting at top left of chart, link flowers tog with ch.

Main chain Join yarn to centre of WS of flower fastener, make 58ch, miss 10ch, ss in next ch to form fastening loop. Do not fasten off.

Join flowers:

First side *2ch, ss in back of a flower A, 2ch, miss 3ch of main chain, ss in next ch of main chain, 3ch, ss in back of a flower B, 3ch, miss next 3ch of main chain, ss in next ch of main ch, rep from * until 6 of flower A and 5 of flower B have been joined.

Second side Now work back along other side of main ch, noting that each ss is worked into the same ch as a ss on first side. **3ch, ss in back of a flower B, 3ch, miss 3ch of main chain, ss in next ch of main chain, 2ch, ss in back of a flower A, 2ch, miss next 3ch of main chain, ss in next ch of main ch, rep from ** until all flowers have been joined. Fasten off.

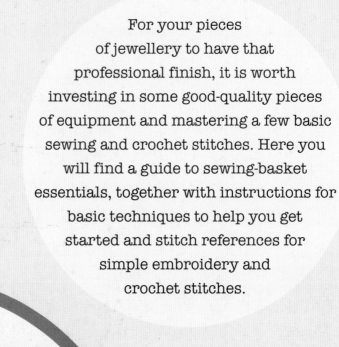

For your pieces of jewellery to have that professional finish, it is worth investing in some good-quality pieces of equipment and mastering a few basic sewing and crochet stitches. Here you will find a guide to sewing-basket essentials, together with instructions for basic techniques to help you get started and stitch references for simple embroidery and crochet stitches.

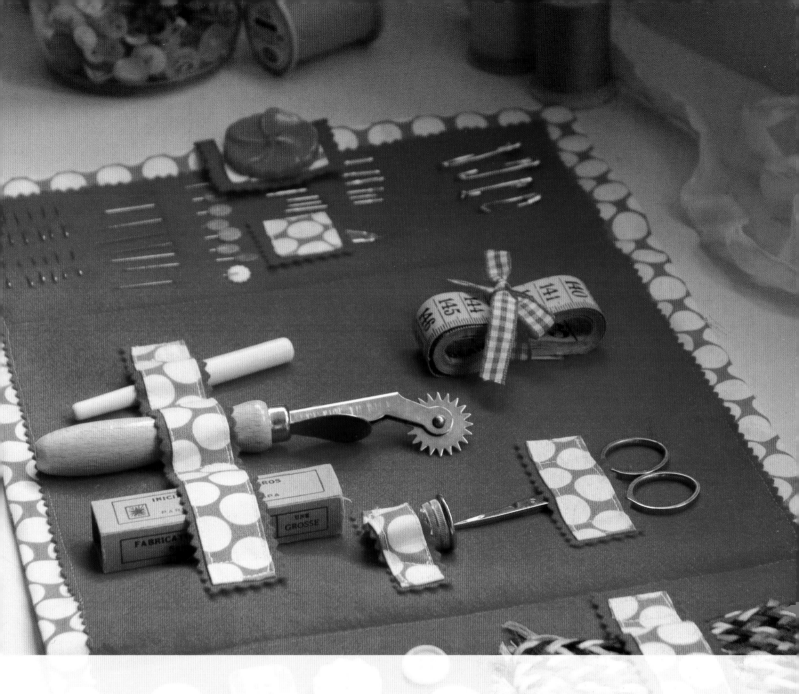

equipment and *techniques*

Equipment

If you are new to sewing and crochet, then you will need to furnish your sewing basket with a few basics to get you started. In addition to the simple tools - needles, scissors, tape measure - your choice of yarns and threads will shape your projects, personalizing them with your own colour schemes. Many of the projects can be adapted as necklaces, bracelets, belts and brooches, and you will even be able to create earrings with the appropriate findings.

Basic sewing kit

Always choose the best quality you can afford for reliable and long-lasting tools. You can always supplement your basic kit, and you will soon be adding to your stash of threads, yarns and beads whenever you visit your craft store.

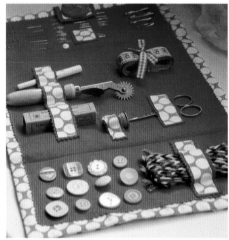

•Scissors
You will need dressmakers' scissors or shears for cutting out fabric, together with a pair of small, sharp embroidery scissors for cutting threads and smaller pieces of fabric. Keep a separate pair of scissors for cutting paper or card templates, as paper can blunt the blades, making it difficult to cut fabric accurately.

•Needles and pins
Use general sewing needles for stitching seams and embroidery needles for embellishing pieces with embroidery stitches and for threading some of the projects together. Keep pins to hand for holding fabrics in place prior to sewing.

•Sewing threads

Cotton sewing threads are available in an infinite variety of colours to match any fabric or yarn. They are suitable for tacking fabrics together prior to sewing or embellishing, and for sewing seams or attaching beads.

•Embroidery threads

Available in different counts, embroidery threads have a wonderful, silky texture and appearance that looks beautiful when used for crochet projects and are strong enough to make a necklace chain, whether chain stitched or knotted together with beads. Stranded embroidery thread, a heavier thread, is perfect for adding embellishments and decorative stitches. Pearl cotton thread is particularly suited to crochet projects since it is non-divisible and fairly thin. It comes in three weights: No. 8 (finest), No. 5 and No. 3 (heaviest).

•Yarns

Wool yarns have a wonderful warm texture and depth of colour that adds a different dimension to jewellery. Whether used to create fluffy pompoms or crocheted as beads, their characteristics make them very appealing for jewellery work. Other more unconventional yarns, can also be used for jewellery, such as lamé (metallic) yarn and raffia yarn. Raffia yarn is available in 25g hanks, and one hank per colour used will be sufficient for each project in this book.

•Tape measure

For some projects, accurate measuring is essential. A tape measure or ruler should always be to hand for checking measurements and you should use one system of measurement, imperial or metric, never a mixture of both.

•Crochet hooks

Depending on the size, crochet hooks can be made from metal, plastic or wood. Choose a hook that has a smooth point and notch. The instructions for each project give a recommended hook size, but use the conversion chart (right) if required.

Crochet hook conversions

Metric (mm)	US size	UK/Canada (old) Wool	Cotton
0.60	No. 14 steel	-	7
0.75	No. 12 steel	-	6½
1.00	No. 10 steel	-	5½
1.25	No. 9 steel	-	4½
1.50	No. 8 steel	16	3½
1.75	No. 7 steel	15	2½
2.00	B/1	14	1½
2.50	C/2	12	0
3.00	D/3	11	3
3.50	E/4	9	4
4.00	F/5	8	5
4.50	G/6	7	
5.00	H/8	6	
5.50	I/9	5	
6.00	J/10	4	
6.50	K10½	3	
7.00	K10½	2	
8.00	L/12	0	
9.00	M/13	00	
10.00	N/15	000	
12.00	N/15	000	
15.00	N/15	000	
17.00	N/15	000	
25.00	N/15	000	
35.00	N/15	000	

Embellishments

In addition to the effects that you can achieve
with a needle and thread, you can embellish
your work with beads and other decorations
that are readily available from your craft store.
Choose from cut glass to tiny seed beads and
semi-precious stones.

Techniques: Making pompoms

Pompoms are simple (and very therapeutic!) to make and can be used for all sorts of embellishments, from bracelets and necklaces, to belts, bag charms, brooches and hair clips.

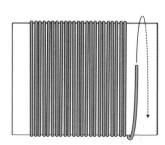 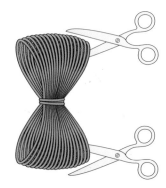 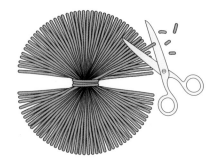

1 Wrap the yarn around a rectangle of stiff card or cardboard, slightly deeper than the required finished pompom diameter. Make 45 wrapped loops around the card.

2 Slip the yarn off the card and wrap a length of matching yarn around the centre, tying tightly. Cut the top and bottom loops of yarn.

3 Fluff out the pompom and neaten any protruding strands.

Techniques: Making beaded tassels

These tassels are incredibly versatile. They make a bold statement as a ring or necklace (see page 56), or can be used to make a belt, or decorate a wrap or scarf.

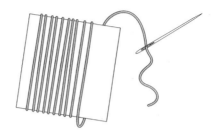

1 Wrap the yarn around a rectangle of stiff card or cardboard, slightly deeper than the required finished pompom diameter. Make 45 wrapped loops around the card.

2 Slip the yarn off the card and wrap the thread end around the top loops several times. Tie tightly to bind the strands together. Leave the long end of thread.

3 In a contrasting colour, if required, wrap yarn around the top of the loops, then stitch over the threads, bringing the needle over and behind the threads to make a stitch. Secure the thread and trim any excess.

4 To make a beaded tassel, attach a length of beading thread to the top band of yarn. Thread on several small beads to make a full circle around the yarn. Bring the needle back through the first and last two beads to secure together and thread through the tassel to secure in place.

5 Repeat Step 4 for the base of the band. Cut the bottom loops of yarn and trim any ends if necessary.

Techniques: Making a ring clasp

Several of the necklaces and bracelets in the projects are secured with a clasp made from matching embroidery yarn. Created with a few loops secured with blanket stitch, these are the perfect way to finish your jewellery pieces.

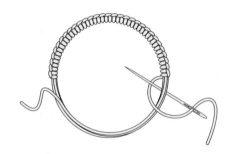

1 Make two or three loops of yarn, and leave the tail end of the yarn.

2 Thread a needle with matching yarn and blanket stitch the loops together (see page 107). To reinforce the ring, pull the tail end of the loop of yarn to bring the stitches together. Secure the thread and trim the excess. The clasp can now be attached to a bracelet or necklace chain.

Stitch library

Embroidery stitches

There is an incredible range of embroidery stitches at your disposal for decorating your jewellery pieces. Either work them on a base, such as the embroidered flowers on pages 20–27, or use them as added decoration and texture, such as the combinations of French knots and seed beads on the beaded collar on page 44.

French knots

Bring out the needle where you would like to position the knot. Encircle the needle two or three times with the thread, then turn the needle back to reinsert it just above where it first emerged. Holding the thread taut with your left hand or thumb, pull the thread through to the back of the work or bring it up again where you want to position the next stitch.

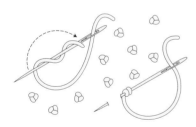

Satin stitch

Work straight stitches closely together across the shape to fill the area required. Keep the edge even and if you are following an outline marked on the fabric, take the stitches outside the line so that the marked line does not show.

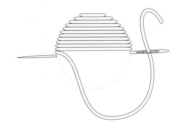

Blanket stitch

Work from left to right. Bring the thread out on the edge. Insert the needle above and to the right of this point, bringing it out vertically straight down with the thread under the tip of the needle. Pull up the stitch to form the loop and repeat.

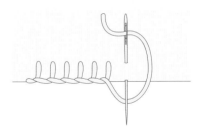

Running stitch

Take several small, even stitches at one time before pulling the thread through.

Crochet stitches

Crochet stitches are all made in a similar way. Apart from slip stitch and chain stitch, the basic crochet stitches vary in height, which is determined by the number of times the yarn is wrapped around the hook.

Crochet is a two-handed craft, with the left hand tensioning the yarn and holding the work while the right hand uses the hook. Because the left hand does a lot of work, most left-handed people find that they are comfortable working this way but if preferred, left-handers could reverse the actions, reading left for right and right for left, using a mirror if necessary to check the illustrations.

Making a slip knot
A slip knot is needed to start some of the projects. It is not counted as a stitch.

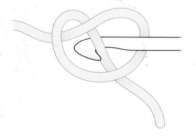

1 Make a loop in the yarn, insert the hook and catch the back strand of the yarn.

2 Pull a loop through, then gently pull on both ends to tighten the knot and close the loop on the hook.

Abbreviations

beg	begin(ning)
ch	chain
cm	centimetres
dc	double crochet
dtr	double treble
htr	half treble
in	inches
rep	repeat
RS	right side
ss	slip stitch
st(s)	stitch(es)
tog	together
tr	treble
ttr	triple treble
WS	wrong side

Chain stitch

Chain stitch may be used as a foundation for other stitches or as a strand to join beads or elements of a necklace.

1 With the hook in front of the yarn, dip the tip to take the yarn over the hook from the back to the front and catch the yarn. This is called yarn over hook and is a basic movement for all crochet stitches.

2 Bring the yarn through the loop on the hook to make a new chain loop on the hook.

Slip stitch

This is the shortest stitch, used for joining stitches, to work to a new place in a pattern or to make a decorative surface chain.

1 Insert the hook into stitch and wrap yarn over hook. Draw a new loop through both the stitch and the loop on the hook, so ending with one loop on the hook.

Double crochet

This is made in the same way as a slip stitch but with an extra stage, giving a stitch that is almost square.

1 Insert the hook into chain or stitch indicated in the instructions, yarn over hook and draw the yarn through the stitch to make two loops on tthe hook.

2 Yarn over hook and draw through two loops on hook, so ending with one loop on the hook.

Treble crochet

Wrapping the yarn around before inserting the hook makes a longer stitch.

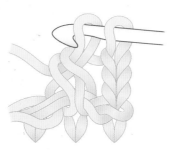 

1 Yarn over hook, insert hook into chain or stitch indicated in the instructions. Yarn over hook, pull through the stitch to make three loops on the hook. Yarn over hook, pull through the first two loops on the hook, so making two loops on the hook.

2 Take the yarn over the hook again and pull through the two loops, so ending with one loop on the hook.

Half treble crochet

This is made in the same way as treble crochet but the stitch is shorter.

1 Work as for treble crochet until there are three loops on the hook. Yarn over hook and draw through three loops on hook, so ending with one loop on the hook.

Working longer stitches

Longer stitches are worked in the same way as a treble but with one more wrapping of the yarn around the hook at the start, so giving one more step when drawing through two loops at a time. Work these stitches as follows:

Double treble: Wrap the yarn round the hook twice and insert in the 5th chain from the hook, yarn around hook and pull through so you have four loops on the hook. Take the yarn around the hook again and pull through 2 loops; repeat three times until you are back to one loop on the hook.

Triple treble: Wrap the yarn round the hook three times and insert in the 6th chain from the hook, yarn around hook and pull through so you have five loops on the hook. Take the yarn around the hook again and pull through 2 loops; repeat four times until you are back to one loop on the hook.

Tips for beginners

Working the stitches

If you've never tried crochet before, use a smooth, medium-weight, light-coloured yarn and a medium-sized hook to try out the basic stitches given on these pages before starting a project.

Holding the hook

Hold the hook like a pencil with the shaft above your hand. Your grip should be light so that you can easily extend the hook in a forwards and back motion.

Holding the yarn

Make a slip knot on the hook, then catch the yarn that goes to the ball around the little finger of the left hand. Bring the hook towards you to take the yarn over the fingers and hold the tail end of yarn from the slip knot between first finger and thumb. Extend the middle finger to make a space for the hook to catch the yarn. As you make stitches, allow the yarn to ease through the fingers and move the work to keep a grip near the place that a new stitch will be made. If working with fine or slippery yarn, wrap the yarn more times around the middle finger.

Templates

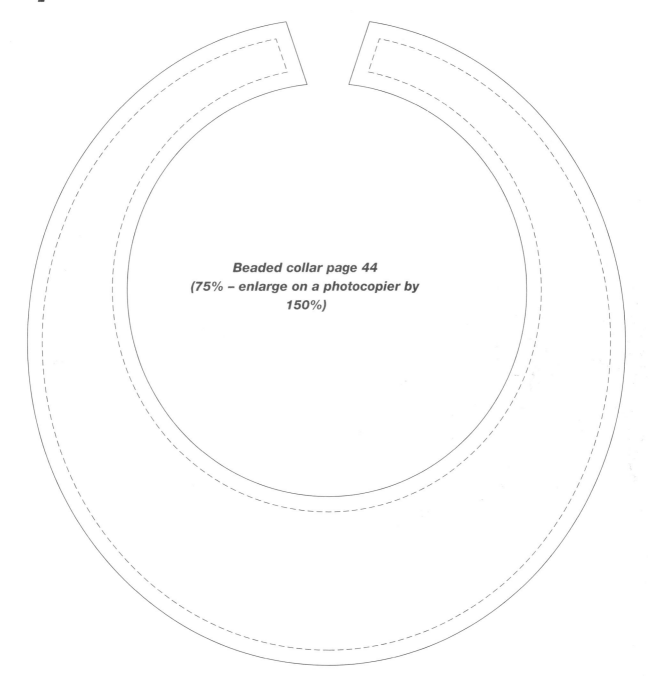

Beaded collar page 44
(75% – enlarge on a photocopier by
150%)

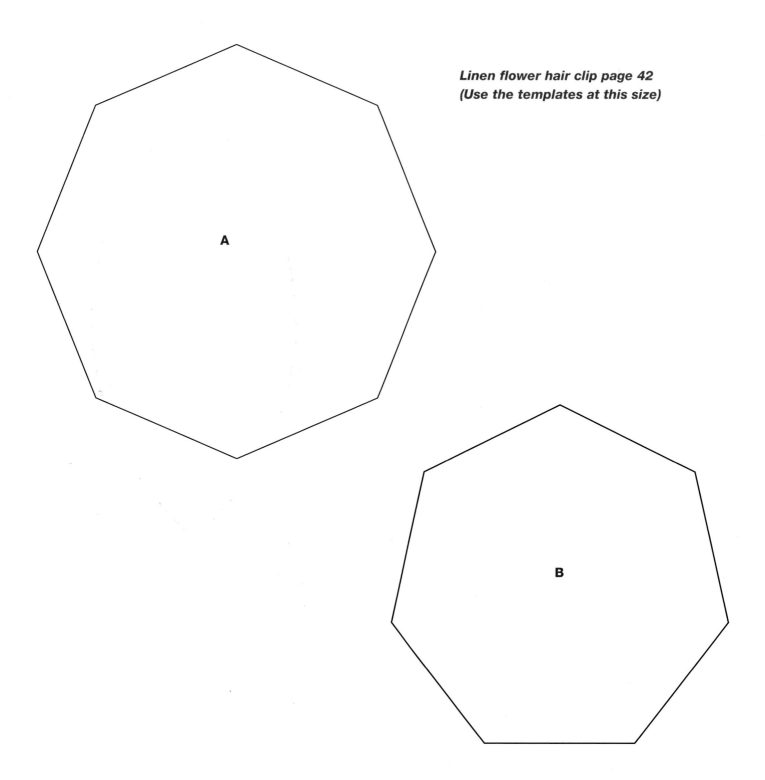

A

Linen flower hair clip page 42
(Use the templates at this size)

B

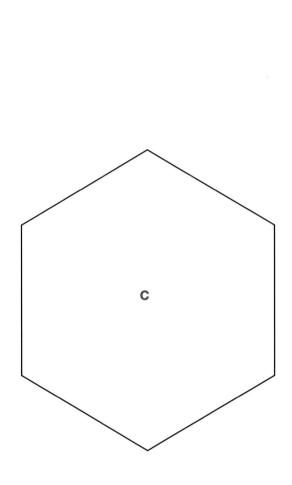

C

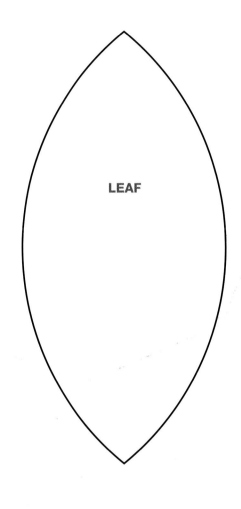

LEAF

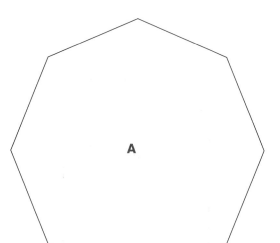

Linen flower necklace page 40
(Use the templates at this size)

A

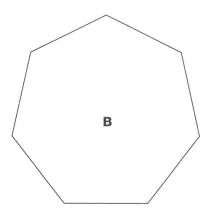

B

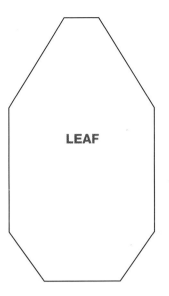

LEAF

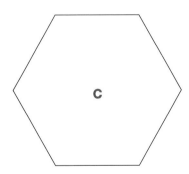

C

SUPPLIERS

Yarns

US
Debbie Bliss, Noro, and Sirdar
Knitting Fever, Inc.
315 Bayview Avenue
Amityville, NY 11701
tel: 516 546 3600
www.knittingfever.com

Rowan
Rowan USA
4 Townsend West
Suite 8
Nashua, NH 03064
tel: 603 886 5041/5043

Canada
Debbie Bliss and Sirdar
Diamond Yarns
155 Martin Ross Avenue, Unit 3
Toronto, ON M3J 2L9
tel: 416 736 6111
www.diamondyarn.com

Australia
Debbie Bliss and Noro
Prestige Yarns (PTY) Ltd.
PO Box 39
Bulli, NSW 2516
tel: 02 4285 6669
www.prestigeyarns.com

Rowan
Cottonfields Crafts and Yarns
263 Stirling Highway
Claremont, WA 6010
tel: 08 9383 4410
www.cottonfields.net.au

Sunspun
185 Canterbury Road
Canterbury, VIC 3126
tel: 03 9830 1609
www.sunspun.com.au

New Zealand
Rowan
Knit World
PO Box 30 645
Lower Hutt
tel: 04 586 4530
www.knitting.co.nz

UK
Debbie Bliss and Noro
Designer Yarns
Units 8–10
Newbridge Industrial Estate
Pitt Street
Keighley
West Yorkshire BD21 4PQ
tel: 01535 664222
www.designeryarns.uk.com

Rowan
Rowan Yarns
Green Lane Mill
Holmfirth
West Yorkshire HD9 2DX
tel: 01484 681881
www.knitrowan.com
www.coatscrafts.co.uk

Sirdar
Sirdar Spinning Ltd
Flanshaw Lane
Alverthorpe
Wakefield
West Yorkshire WE2 9ND
www.sirdar.co.uk

DMC embroidery threads
www.dmc.com

Emi Iwakiri's crochet kits are
available from
www.hobbyra-hobbyre.com

Beads and embellishments

US

Beadalon
205 Carter Drive
West Chester, PA 19382
tel: 866 423 2325
www.beadalon.com

Crystal Innovations/Pure Allure, Inc.
4005 Avenida De la Plata
Oceanside, CA 92056
tel: 800 536 6312
www.pureallure.com

Fire Mountain Gems and Beads
1 Fire Mountain Way
Grants Pass, OR 97526
tel: 800 355 2137
www.firemountaingems.com

Great Craft Works
133 West Gay Street
West Chester, PA 19380
tel: 888 811 5773

Hirschberg Schutz and Co.
650 Liberty Avenue
Union, NJ 07083
tel: 908 810 1111

Marvin Schwab, The Bead
Warehouse
2740 Garfield Avenue
Silver Spring, MD 20910
tel: 301 565 0487
www.thebeadwarehouse.com

Phoenix Beads, Jewelry and Parts
5 West 37th Street
New York, NY 10018
tel: 212 278 8688
www.phoenixbeads.com

Rings and Things
PO Box 450
Spokane, WA 99210
tel: 800 336 2156
www.rings-things.com

Swarovski North America Limited
1 Kenney Drive
Cranston, RI 02920
tel: 800 463 0849
www.swarovski.com

UK

Bead Addict
www.beadaddict.co.uk

Bead Aura
3 Neals Yard
London WC2H 9DP
tel: 020 7836 3002
www.beadaura.co.uk

Beads Direct
www.beadsdirect.co.uk

Bead Shop
21A Tower Street
London WC2 9NS
tel: 020 7240 0931
www.beadshop.co.uk

Bijoux Beads
Elton House
2 Abbey Street
Bath BA1 1NN
tel: 01225 482024
www.bijouxbeads.co.uk

Crystals
www.crystalshop.co.uk

London Bead Company
339 Kentish Town Road
London NW5 2TJ
tel: 0870 203 2323
www.londonbeadco.co.uk

Spangles 4 Beads
www.spangles4beads.co.uk

INDEX

Acknowledgements

I would like to acknowledge the generosity and kindness of my family, Takashi, my husband, Taisuke, my son, Momo, my daughter and Kiri, my dog, who shared parts of their lives to help me for this book. Katsura, my mother, who encouraged me to explore new opportunities and Kikue, my grandmother, who inspired me with crochet and textile work and gave me all her skills. I really appreciate the help of Michie Takatsuki, who helped me to make the pieces. I am truly grateful to Kei Hirano who loves my work and made this opportunity possible. Big thanks to Cindy Richards for commissioning the book and Becky Maynes for her beautiful photographs. Thanks to Sally Powell and Luis Peral-Aranda for the lovely design, Katie Hardwicke for editing the text and all the wonderful people behind the scenes at CICO Books. This book was made by all of your dedication.